FEEDING YOURSELF

VICKI COBB
Pictures by Marylin Hafner

HODDER AND STOUGHTON
LONDON SYDNEY AUCKLAND TORONTO

British Library in Cataloguing Publication Data

Cobb, Vicki, *1938-*
Feeding yourself.
1. Cutlery, history
I. Title   II. Hafner, Marilyn
638.82

ISBN 0-340-52674-2

First published 1989 by J B Lippincott, New York
First published in Great Britain 1990

Published by Hodder and Stoughton Children's Books,
a division of Hodder and Stoughton Ltd,
Mill Road, Dunton Green, Sevenoaks, Kent TN13 2YA

Printed in Italy by New Interlitho, Milan

Time for dinner. What are you having? Maybe it's soup, or steak and mashed potatoes, or stir-fried vegetables. Suppose you didn't have a knife, fork, pair of chopsticks, or a spoon.

In some parts of the world it's polite to eat with your fingers all the time. But for preparing meals and eating many kinds of dishes, tools are useful inventions.

People did not always use eating tools. About five hundred years ago, food was put out on platters in the middle of the table. Each person used a large, hard cracker called a *trencher* as a plate. Gravy made the trenchers soggy, so extra trenchers were put on the table. People took food from the platters with their fingers and put it on their trenchers.

No one knows who invented the knife, fork, chopsticks, or spoon. But they have been used to prepare food and to get it to your mouth for centuries. Here are their stories.

THE KNIFE

Thousands of years ago, people lived in caves. When a caveman wanted to crack open a nut, he smashed it with a rock. The rock became a kind of hammer. Then someone must have discovered that if the hammer had a sharp edge, it could cut wood. And so the axe was invented.

A small stone with a sharp edge could be used to cut things that were softer than wood. Such a small, sharp stone became the first knife.

Cavemen worked out which were the best kinds of stones for making knives and all sorts of cutting tools. Cavemen made so many different kinds of tools from stones that we call the time they lived in the Stone Age.

Thousands of years later, people discovered how to use metals such as bronze and iron. Metal was stronger than stone and could be made into many more shapes. Knives began to look more like the knives we use now.

Soon everyone carried a knife. It was the all-purpose eating tool.

Two hundred years ago people began setting the table with a knife for each person. A table knife can be used in several ways, for example spreading jam and cutting food into bite-sized pieces.

THE FORK

The first fork was probably a pointed stick. You've used the earliest kind of fork if you've ever roasted a marshmallow over a camp fire. You also know there can be problems. Your marshmallow may fall off.

Why not make a tool with more than one point? With two points there is a better chance of holding speared food. A fork that had two points, or prongs, was invented by the Romans. They used their fork for cooking. The word *fork* has come to mean 'divide into two or more branches'.

Although people have used forks for cooking for thousands of years, they have only been eating with them for the last two centuries.

About five hundred years ago, some kings and queens put forks on their tables. But people who first used a fork at dinner were thought to be very strange.

A two-pronged fork is only good for spearing food. Today's table fork has four prongs. The four prongs close together keep food from slipping between the cracks. So you can use a table fork to scoop up food, like a spoon.

A fork and knife together make a great team for cutting meat. Most people stab the meat and hold it still with the fork in their left hand and saw away with the knife in their right.

In most countries of the world, people lift the meat to the mouth with their left hand as soon as it is cut. But Americans put down the knife and then move the fork to their right hand before lifting the food to their mouth.

CONFUSING ISN'T IT?

CHOPSTICKS

There's only one easy way to pick up a pea with your fingers. You use your thumb and your index finger like pincers. The pea can be neatly lifted to your mouth. Now suppose you want to pick up a pea without touching it with your fingers. Thousands of years ago, the Chinese invented just the tool to do this: chopsticks.

Chopsticks are simply two slim sticks about as long as a man's hand. Chinese chopsticks have blunt ends. Japanese chopsticks are slimmer and have pointed ends.

CHINESE

JAPANESE

I WONDER IF I COULD LEARN TO USE THOSE.

Millions of Asian people use chopsticks instead of knives and forks. Chinese and Japanese children all learn how, just as Western children learn to use a knife and fork.

Everyone can learn to use chopsticks. If you don't have chopsticks handy, you can practise with two pencils.

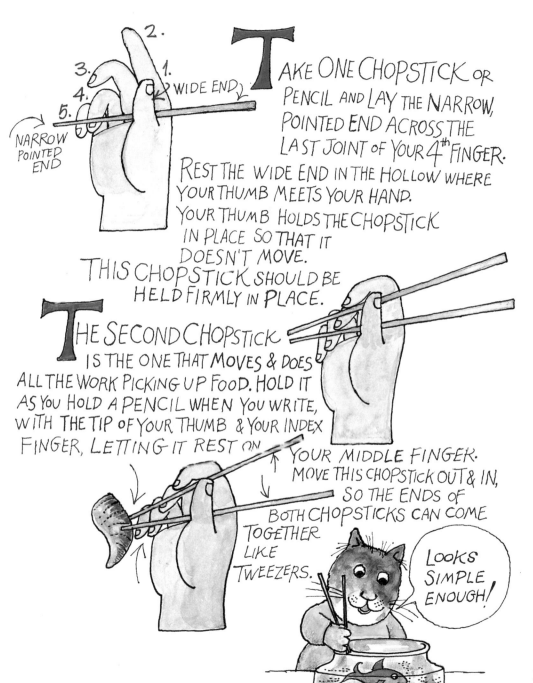

TAKE ONE CHOPSTICK OR PENCIL AND LAY THE NARROW, POINTED END ACROSS THE LAST JOINT OF YOUR 4th FINGER. REST THE WIDE END IN THE HOLLOW WHERE YOUR THUMB MEETS YOUR HAND. YOUR THUMB HOLDS THE CHOPSTICK IN PLACE SO THAT IT DOESN'T MOVE. THIS CHOPSTICK SHOULD BE HELD FIRMLY IN PLACE.

THE SECOND CHOPSTICK IS THE ONE THAT MOVES & DOES ALL THE WORK PICKING UP FOOD. HOLD IT AS YOU HOLD A PENCIL WHEN YOU WRITE, WITH THE TIP OF YOUR THUMB & YOUR INDEX FINGER, LETTING IT REST ON YOUR MIDDLE FINGER. MOVE THIS CHOPSTICK OUT & IN, SO THE ENDS OF BOTH CHOPSTICKS CAN COME TOGETHER LIKE TWEEZERS.

WIDE END

NARROW POINTED END

LOOKS SIMPLE ENOUGH!

Practise picking up small objects, and pretty soon you will become comfortable using your chopsticks. From time to time, you may have to tap the ends of both chopsticks to keep them even.

Most Asian food is already cut into small pieces when it's brought to the table, so knives are not needed.

Chinese restaurants will give you chopsticks if you ask. It feels right to eat Chinese and Japanese food with chopsticks, not forks.

Chopstick experts can eat very quickly.

The word *chopsticks* means 'fast sticks'.

THE SPOON

Imagine trying to drink from a stream. You cup your hands and use them as a bowl to carry the water to your mouth.

People need bowls to carry liquids. A knife or fork or chopsticks simply won't do.

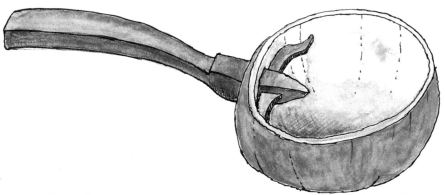

The first spoon-users put a small bowl at the end of a handle. This tool could dish up liquids by the mouthful. It could stir soups and scoop up a small bit for tasting.

IT SMELLS GOOD!

The spoon is one of the earliest tools ever invented. It is used all over the world.

Spoons come in many different sizes and shapes to do different jobs.

ICE CREAM SODA SPOON

LADLE

TEASPOON

MEASURING SPOONS

TABLESPOON

WOODEN
SPOON

KITCHEN
SPOONS

GRAPEFRUIT
SPOON
WITH
SERRATED
TIP

SLOTTED
SPOON

SERVING SPOON

SOUP
SPOON

31

Eating tools are perfect for the jobs they have to do. How clever people were to invent them!